Speak for Yourself

To get the complete **Idioms for Inclusivity** experience, this book can be purchased alongside four others as a set, ***Idioms for Inclusivity: Fostering Belonging with Language, 978-1-032-28635-8***.

Informed by sociolinguistic research, yet written accessibly, *Speak for Yourself* challenges readers to investigate the concept of assumptions as it relates to both language-use and inclusivity.

This engaging and delightfully illustrated book invites students to engage with concepts such as:

- the cultural meaning of the idiom "speak for yourself"

- presuppositions – a concept developed by linguists to research and understand assumptions in language

- how "Speak for Yourself" can be a helpful warning against harmful assumptions

- how understanding the way language works can help us learn to be more inclusive

Featuring practical inclusivity tips related to integrating learning into daily conversations, this enriching curriculum supplement can be used in a Language Arts setting to learn about figurative language; in a Social Studies setting to discuss diversity, equity, inclusion, and belonging; or as an introduction to linguistics for students ages 7–14.

Samantha Beaver is a workplace communications analyst and linguist. She has been involved in language research and teaching/training since 2013. She is currently CEO and Founder of Memra Language Services.

SPEAK FOR YOURSELF

DISCUSSING ASSUMPTIONS

SAMANTHA BEAVER

ILLUSTRATED BY
MELISSA LEE JOHNSON

Routledge
Taylor & Francis Group

NEW YORK AND LONDON

Designed cover image: Illustrated by Melissa Lee Johnson

First published 2023
by Routledge
605 Third Avenue, New York, NY 10158

and by Routledge
4 Park Square, Milton Park, Abingdon, Oxon, OX14 4RN

Routledge is an imprint of the Taylor & Francis Group, an informa business

ISBN: 978-1-032-29344-8 (hbk)
ISBN: 978-1-032-28638-9 (pbk)
ISBN: 978-1-003-30116-5 (ebk)

DOI: 10.4324/9781003301165

Typeset in Futura
by Deanta Global Publishing Services, Chennai, India

Contents

CHAPTER 1

About This Book

DOI: 10.4324/9781003301165-1

The Language Idioms for Inclusivity series is a collection of short, illustrated books for ages 7–14 that use common language idioms/expressions to explore concepts related to inclusivity. This exploration is informed by sociolinguistic and pragmatic research but is written in a readable format, wherein the author poses probing questions to the reader and guides them through linguistic analysis by suggesting possible answers.

This series introduces children to key concepts in linguistics and gives them (and their parents or instructors) a new, language-oriented framework to use when discussing issues of inclusion.

Speak for Yourself: Discussing Assumptions is the fifth installment in the Language Idioms for Inclusivity series. In this book, the author challenges readers to investigate assumptions as they relate to both language-use and inclusivity. The author does this by (1) explaining the cultural meaning of the idiom, "speak for yourself"; (2) introducing presuppositions, a concept developed by linguists use to research and understand assumptions in language; and (3) explaining why hearing the idiom "speak for yourself" can act as a helpful warning against making harmful assumptions. The book ends with a description of how understanding the way language works can help us be more inclusive and practical language tips to integrate learning into daily conversations.

As a supplement to traditional curriculum, this book can be used in a Language Arts setting to learn about figurative language; in a Social Studies setting to discuss diversity, equity, inclusion, and belonging; or as an introduction to linguistics, a college-level subject that is not typically offered to K–12 students.

CHAPTER 2

How to Use This Book in Your Teaching Practice

DOI: 10.4324/9781003301165-2

In whichever context you choose to read this book, here are some suggestions for integrating it into teaching.

1. *Always Aloud, Always Together*

When using it in the classroom or at home, read this book aloud with your 7–14-year-old. The concepts in this book are new and abstract, but the tone of the book speaks to a middle-school audience. Likewise, the illustrations are meant to be seen and enhance the intended learning. Experiencing this book together connects the teacher and learner in a way that promotes questioning, critical thinking, and side-by-side learning. These ideas might be just as new for you as they are for your students! What a wonderful opportunity to learn together.

2. *Use Yourself As An Example*

Familiarize yourself with the book before using it in the classroom. After reading through the concepts and examples, try to think of some real language examples from conversations that you've experienced that reflect the intended learning. Be vulnerable and tell your students about a time when you felt like someone was making a false assumption about you. By using real examples from your real life, you will extend the feeling that this is a mutual learning experience – and an ongoing one! We are never done learning how to communicate with one another. Your students will feel respected and honored that you are placing yourself in the position of "learner" with them.

3. *Reflect in Discussion*

The intended learnings in this book can be practiced and integrated well into discussion-based activities. Some ideas:

- On notecards, write examples of common assumptions that students might make about one another (ie, "they know how to swim" or "their family owns a car," or "they like spicy food"). Also on note cards, describe different types of people ("your mom," "a 15-year-old hispanic boy," etc). In groups, ask students to pull out one assumption card and one person card. Have them discuss whether they would be likely to make that assumption about that person. Why or why not? Would their parents make the same assumptions that they would? Why or why not?

- Using the Practical Language Tips at the back of this book, ask students to practice having clarifying and inclusive conversations.

4. *Reflect in Writing*

The intended lessons in this series can be practiced and integrated well into writing-based activities. Some ideas:

- Have students create a Belonging Journal. Give weekly writing prompts and allow for 10–15 minutes of writing time for self-reflection. Prompts should offer a range writing-types, including, but not limited to:

  o Brainstorming (list all the assumptions someone might make about you if they heard you talk, but couldn't see you (ie, that I'm a girl, that I'm from a small town, that I eat meat, etc)).

  o Self-reflection (write about a time when a teacher or parent made an assumption about you that was wrong. What assumption did they make? What do you think caused them to assume that about you? How did it feel?).

  o Creative writing (create a world where your brain couldn't make any assumptions at all. How would things be different? Imagine you are at a party. What would meeting new people be like?).

- Have students write an editorial essay. Ask them to share their opinion on an idea or topic presented in this book. Do they agree? Do they disagree? What about their cultural and family background influences what they think? Do they think their friends would agree with them? Their grandparents? Why or why not?

5. *Reflect in Hypothetical Thinking*

The intended lessons in this book can be practiced and integrated well into critical-thinking activities (which can be realized in writing or in discussion). Some ideas:

- Create a character that has different diverse traits. Challenge students to make three different assumptions about that person and explain why they would assume that. Ask each student to choose which assumption they would make first in real life. Ask them why and whether that is a good or bad thing.

- Ask students to imagine a hypothetical world (or school) where every assumption that anyone makes automatically becomes true about that person. How would your identity be different in this world? Are you still yourself? Do you feel free or limited by the assumptions that are being made about you? Why or why not?

Thank you for choosing this book and engaging with these ideas. For more ideas about or support in using linguistics and inclusivity in the classroom, visit www.mem ralanguageservices.com.

CHAPTER 3

Glossary

DOI: 10.4324/9781003301165-3

abstract – when something exists as a thought or idea but not in a physical form.

(to) assume/to make an assumption – to take something as true when there is little or no evidence.

concrete – when something exists in a physical form.

honorable – when something is deserving of respect or honor.

hypothesis – an educated guess that can be tested using the scientific method.

idiomatic expression – a well-known phrase that carries a well-known cultural meaning.

linguists – language scientists; people who study how human language works, both in the brain and out in the world.

presuppositions – ideas or facts, that we take for granted as factual, and that we communicate to one another when we talk – without saying them out loud.

stereotype – a common cultural image or idea about a person or group of people that is usually overly simplified or inaccurate.

CHAPTER 4

The Idiom

DOI: 10.4324/9781003301165-4

What does it mean when someone says, "SPEAK FOR YOURSELF!"?

SPEAK FOR YOURSELF is a phrase you've probably heard your parents or teachers use. Maybe you've even used this phrase yourself.

Usually, this phrase is used in conversations like this one:

Friend A: "Vegan mac and cheese is awesome!"

Friend B: "Ugh, speak for yourself!"

When someone says, "SPEAK FOR YOURSELF," they are using an **idiomatic expression**. An idiomatic expression is a well-known phrase that carries a well-known cultural meaning. The words in an idiomatic phrase don't always make sense if you think about them outside of your cultural context.

For example, when someone says, "Time to hit the hay!," you know that they mean they *need to go to sleep* – even though the actual words "hit the hay" don't mean that on their own. There are lots of idioms in every language and idioms can tell us a lot about the people who speak that language.

In this book we are talking about the idiom, "SPEAK FOR YOURSELF!"

When someone says SPEAK FOR YOURSELF, what they really mean is something like, "your words don't represent me and my opinions."

"Speak for yourself!" reminds another speaker that even though they might make a broad claim, their words reflect and represent only THEM (and not you). Another way to think about SPEAK FOR YOURSELF is that it is a warning against **making assumptions**.

To assume means to take something as true when there is little or no evidence.

Humans make assumptions a lot when we speak. Where do assumptions show up in our language? How does language-use expose the assumptions that we make?

CHAPTER 5

The Linguistic Theory

DOI: 10.4324/9781003301165-5

Language experts, called **linguists**, have thought and argued about this question a lot. Many of them have come up with guesses, also called **hypotheses**, about how language relates to making assumptions. One well-known way to think about language and assumptions in linguistics is called

Presuppositions

Presuppositions are beliefs that we communicate to one another when we talk – without actually saying them out loud.

For example, if you say: "When did Jo stop wearing their helmet?," you are communicating two beliefs that you have about Jo:

(1) That Jo has a helmet.

(2) That Jo wore a helmet at some point in the past.

These beliefs are presuppositions. You didn't say them out loud, but you communicated them by the way you asked the question.

Not every sentence contains presuppositions. You could have said: "Does Jo wear a helmet?" or "I don't think Jo wears a helmet." Both of these sentences have similar meanings to what you said, but they *do not* contain presuppositions about Jo.

Presuppositions are how assumptions show up in language.

Assumptions and presuppositions are two ways to realize the same thing: they both involve judging something to be true.

There IS a difference between assumptions and presuppositions, though.

Assumptions are **abstract** → they only exist in your mind.

Presuppositions are **concrete** → they exist in the sentences that you say.

This difference is very important. It can be hard to fully understand something that only exists in your mind, but it is much easier to understand something that exists out in the world.

Often, the only way to become aware of all the assumptions we make is to look for evidence of them in the presuppositions that show up in our sentences.

Presuppositions can lead to exclusion. This happens when we make *false* assumptions   or when we think something is true, but it's actually not

When we make false assumptions about people, it can be hurtful. And even worse, when we keep making those same false assumptions over and over again, they often turn into **stereotypes**.

Here is an example of how presuppositions can contribute to stereotyping.

1. *Brady says, "Hey Carlos, when are you going to bring some chips and salsa over?!"*

    Presupposition (1) Carlos has easy access to chips and salsa

    (possible) underlying assumptions:

    - Carlos is Mexican American

    - Carlos likes, has, or knows about chips and salsa

    - Carlos is a valuable friend because he has access to chips and salsa

    Presupposition (2) Carlos is going to come over

    (possible) underlying assumptions:

    - Carlos feels invited to come over

    - Carlos wants to come over

    - Carlos is able to come over

In this example, Brady unintentionally contributed to stereotypes about Hispanic Americans, cultural food, and cultural hospitality. How did this happen? Brady had already made some assumptions about Carlos, and so when Brady opened his mouth to speak, those assumptions came out in the form of presuppositions.

How do you think Carlos felt when he heard Brady say, *"Hey Carlos, when are you going to bring some chips and salsa over?!"*?

Carlos probably felt like Brady doesn't truly know him or care to get to know him. And this makes Carlos feel like he doesn't belong.

Our minds like to sort things into categories. Brady is sorting Carlos into a mental category that he has for all Hispanic Americans. This is a problem, because either (1) Brady doesn't have enough information about – or experience with – Hispanic Americans to create accurate and **honorable** categories for them in his mind, or (2) he is intentionally using an offensive and inaccurate mental category for Hispanic Americans to be unkind to Carlos.

Either way, he is defaulting to stereotyping.

CHAPTER 6

The Inclusive Solution

DOI: 10.4324/9781003301165-6

But it doesn't always have to be this way.

Knowing how to find presuppositions in our sentences can help us uncover the assumptions we are making about others. And when we uncover these assumptions, it is much easier to prevent stereotyping.

Imagine you sit next to Aisha in the school choir. Aisha is Black. When the choir director starts teaching the choreography for your Spring concert, they say, "And of course Aisha will have to be in the front to show us her moves!" You notice that Aisha doesn't look very happy when they hear that. Why not? What happened?

Because you understand presuppositions, you can uncover the assumption that the choir director just made about Aisha.

Sentence: "And of course Aisha will have to be in the front to show us her moves!"

Presupposition (1) Aisha is a good dancer

Presupposition (2) Aisha likes to dance

(possible) underlying assumptions

- Black people have better rhythm than other groups of people

- Black people like to dance more than other groups of people

You can't change what the choir director said, but – because you understand presuppositions and their underlying assumptions – you CAN understand why that sentence made Aisha feel sad. This means that you can have empathy toward her, which helps create genuine relationships. When you have genuine relationships with people, your brain is less likely to default to stereotyping because it has a lot of accurate data to create an honorable category for your friend.

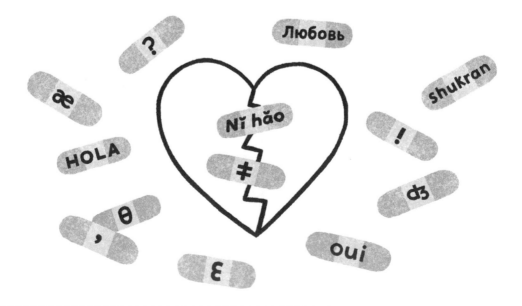

It is easy to imagine Aisha and Carlos thinking, "Speak for yourself!" when the people around them make hurtful assumptions about them (*"Speak for yourself – I don't like to dance in front of people!"* or *"Speak for yourself – it's not my job to bring you chips and salsa!"*)

"SPEAK FOR YOURSELF!" tells us someone is making an assumption based on inaccurate information. But it can also cue us to look for presuppositions in the sentence that we just heard, uncover those assumptions, and build empathy toward others.

Linguistics frees us from stereotyping and gives us the tools to build inclusive relationships.

Linguistics frees us from **STEREOTYPING** *and gives us the tools to build* **INCLUSIVE** *relationships*

CHAPTER 7

Practical Language Tips

DOI: 10.4324/9781003301165-7

When you hear someone make a hurtful assumption about a person or group of people (stereotyping), you might want to argue with them, explaining why they are wrong to assume. Instead of making a *reactionary accusation* ("that's so racist!"), pause and do a quick linguistic analysis of the presuppositions that your opponent made before you say anything. This will help you build a *logical argument*. Your opponent can easily disregard an emotional outburst, but will be encouraged to engage with the evidence from your analysis.

Here are three steps to exposing a stereotype through linguistic analysis.

Step 1: "Collect" the stereotypical sentence. If you can, write it down. If you can't, repeat it to yourself seven times to remember what was said. DO NOT change the sentence – your brain might try to! That is tampering with data and it is bad science. It is also unfair to your opponent.

Example: At the football game, Camilla says, *"Our cheerleading team really needs to lose some weight."*

Step 2: Find the presuppositions. Ask yourself: If this sentence IS TRUE, what also NEEDS to be true? List out your answers.

Example: *(1) the cheerleaders on our cheer team are overweight.*

Step 3: Find the underlying assumptions that created the presuppositions. Ask yourself: if these presuppositions ARE PRESENT, what does the speaker have to believe about the world? List out your answers.

Example: *Camilla believes that (1) in order to "be a cheerleader" you need to be a certain weight (which is not "overweight"), (2) it is bad for cheerleaders to be overweight, (3) overweight cheerleaders should lose weight.*

Now that you have your linguistic analysis, you can build a more general argument. Below are four important parts of every argument. You can remember these parts by putting them into an acronym.

"Take your S. H. O. T."

1. **SOLUTION (share how you would solve the problem → share a non-stereotypical way to rephrase the sentence)**

   a. Example: *Saying it that way is a little stereotypical. A more accurate way would be to say something like, "Some of our cheerleaders have a different body type than other cheerleaders I've seen."*

2. **HARM (share the harm that the stereotypical sentence causes and WHY – list the underlying assumptions first, then list the presuppositions)**

   a. (underlying assumptions) Example: *Saying that cheerleaders need to lose weight implies that you believe that in order to "be a cheerleader" you need to be a certain weight (which is not "overweight"). This could really make someone feel excluded because of their weight!*

      i. at this point, your opponent may or may not deny having these beliefs. Luckily, you have evidence that they DO believe these things in your presuppositions. Continue building your argument calmly.

   b. (presuppositions) Example: *If it is true that, "our cheerleading team really needs to lose weight," as you say, then it also has to be true that (1) the cheerleaders on our cheer team are overweight. And are they? It seems like you simply have a preference for thin cheerleaders, which is based on a stereotypical idea of what a cheerleader should look like.*

3. **OBSTACLE (share the obstacle that prevents stereotypes like this one from changing)**

   a. Example: *Our brains love putting things (and people!) into categories. It makes sense that you have a category for cheerleaders that includes assumptions about weight, because a lot of our ideas about cheerleaders come from popular culture, not real evidence.*

4. **THANKFULNESS (thank your opponent for listening)**

   a. Example: *Thank you for letting me share my perspective!*

Bibliography

Bibliography

Ahearn, L. M. (2021). *Living language: An introduction to linguistic anthropology.* John Wiley & Sons.

Archer, D., Aijmer, K., & Wichmann, A. (2013). *Pragmatics: An advanced resource book for students.* Routledge.

Kameswari, L., Sravani, D., & Mamidi, R. (2020, July). Enhancing bias detection in political news using pragmatic presupposition. In *Proceedings of the Eighth International Workshop on Natural Language Processing for Social Media* (pp. 1–6).

Levinson, S. C., Levinson, S. C., & Levinson, S. (1983). *Pragmatics.* Cambridge University Press.

Lyubymova, S. (2020). Associative experiment in the study of a sociocultural stereotype. *Kalbų Studijos, 36,* 85–96.

Meet the Author and Illustrator

Meet the Author

Samantha Beaver is a linguist. She got her Master's Degree in Applied English Linguistics from the University of Wisconsin-Madison. Sociolinguistics, Pragmatics, and Conversation Analysis are her areas of linguistic expertise, and her favorite topics to explore are language equity, language and gender, language learning, language and people management, and language and power. When she's not doing linguistic work for other people, she is at home fostering the language development of her two sons, Simon and Louis. You can learn more about Samantha's work at www.memralanguageservices.com.

Meet the Illustrator

Melissa Lee Johnson is an award-winning artist, illustrator, and graphic designer. She graduated with a Bachelor of Fine Arts in Integrated Studio Arts from the Milwaukee Institute of Art and Design and got her start illustrating for an alternative newspaper. In 2020 she received the Communication Arts Illustration Annual Award of Excellence in Advertising. She currently works for Made By Things, a small animation studio based in Columbus, Ohio. When she's not drawing, she likes to hang with Bambi, Sparkle, and Trixie, her three rescue Chihuahuas. You can learn more about her at melissaleejohnsonart.com.

Samantha and Melissa became best friends when they were middle schoolers. Even back then, they often imagined teaming up to write and illustrate a book together someday. The content of this book is especially meaningful for them, because it wasn't always easy to remain friends and accept each other's differences and decisions as they grew into adults. A patient persistence has allowed them to hold fast to what now feels like sisterhood, and they hope that readers of this book learn that the best way to love someone who is different from you is to simply *keep trying*.